GOING TO SCHOOL
DURING THE
CIVIL WAR: THE UNION

by Kerry A. Graves

Consultant: Melodie Andrews
Associate Professor of Early American History
Minnesota State University, Mankato

Blue Earth Books

an imprint of Capstone Press
Mankato, Minnesota

Blue Earth Books are published by Capstone Press
151 Good Counsel Drive, P.O. Box 669, Mankato, Minnesota 56002
http://www.capstone-press.com

Library of Congress Cataloging-in-Publication Data
Graves, Kerry A.
   Going to school during the Civil War: the Union / by Kerry A. Graves
   p. cm.—(Going to school in history)
   Includes bibliographical references (p. 31) and index.
   ISBN 0-7368-0801-9
   1. Education—United States—History—19th century—Juvenile literature. 2. United States—History—Civil War, 1861–1865—Juvenile
literature. [1. Education—History—19th century. 2. United States—History—Civil War, 1861–1865.] I. Title. II. Series.
LA215.G72 2002
370'.973—dc21

00-011624

   Summary: Discusses the school life of Northern children at the time of the Civil War, including lessons, books, teachers, examinations, and
special days. Includes activities and sidebars.

Editorial Credits
Editor: Rachel Koestler
Designer and Illustrator: Heather Kindseth
Product Planning Editor: Lois Wallentine
Photo Researchers: Heidi Schoof and Judy Winter

Acknowledgment
Blue Earth Books thanks Charles F. Faust for his assistance with
this book.

Photo Credits
Robert Dennis Collection of Stereoscopic Views, The New York Public
Library, cover, 3 (bottom), 17, 23; Stock Montage, Inc., 3 (top), 6, 28;
Schomburg Center for Research in Black Culture, The New York Public
Library, 14; Photography Collection, Miriam and Ira D. Wallach, New
York Public Library, 8; North Wind Picture Archives, 7, 11 (top), 18, 21,
25; Collection of the New-York Historical Society, 20; Library of
Congress, 11 (bottom), 27 (top); CORBIS, 13, 15, 24 (*First Lessons in
Geography*); Department of Special Collections, Charles E. Young
Research Library, UCLA, 27 (bottom); Charles F. Faust, 12; Gregg
Andersen, 24 (flag), Capstone Press/Gary Sundermeyer, 19, 29

1 2 3 4 5 6 06 07 05 04 03 02

Contents

Preserving the Union

In the mid-1800s, two very different economies and lifestyles divided the United States. The Northern states based their economy on factories, businesses, and small farms. In the South, the economy depended on plantations, where cotton, tobacco, or rice was grown in large fields. These crops had to be tended by hand. Plantation owners depended on African slaves to do this hard, physical labor.

Southern plantation owners used many slaves to operate their plantations. They bought slaves from slave traders who had forced Africans to leave their homes in West Africa. In 1808, slave traders stopped bringing enslaved Africans to the United States. But plantation owners continued to buy and sell American-born Africans.

Slaves had difficult lives. They worked long hours doing hard work. Many slave owners were cruel to their slaves. Slaves received only small rations of food to feed their families. Plantation owners sometimes beat or sold slaves who complained. When plantation owners sold slaves, African families often were separated.

Northerners and Southerners disagreed about slavery. By the early 1800s, most Northerners had ended slavery in their states. But many Southerners argued that they needed slaves for their plantations to succeed. Some Northern abolitionists believed slavery should be illegal in all states.

The United States during the Civil War (1861–1865)

Minnesota

Wisconsin

Michigan

Vermont

Maine

New York

New Hampshire

Iowa

Pennsylvania

Massachusetts

Illinois

Indiana

Ohio

Rhode Island

Connecticut

Kansas

Missouri

West Virginia

Kentucky

Virginia

New Jersey

Delaware

Maryland

Tennessee

North Carolina

Arkansas

South Carolina

Mississippi

Alabama

Georgia

Texas

Louisiana

Florida

Union States

Border States

Confederate States

"We were having our regular literary exercises on Friday afternoon, at our Seminary, when the cry ["The rebels are coming!"] reached our ears. Rushing to the door, and standing on the front portico [porch] we beheld . . . a dark, dense mass, moving toward town. Our teacher, Mrs. Eyster, at once said: 'Children, run home as quickly as you can.'"
—Tillie Pierce, age 15, from At Gettysburg

The North and the South also disagreed over government issues. In the South, people believed each state should have the right to make its own laws on social issues, including slavery. Northerners wanted a strong national government. They felt the federal government should make political and social decisions for the whole country.

The Battle of Gettysburg took place in Pennsylvania from July 1 to July 3, 1863. Pennsylvania was part of the Union.

Abraham Lincoln was elected president in 1860. He supported a strong national government. Many Southerners feared Lincoln would take away states' rights to make their own laws about social issues. Many Southerners began to talk about creating their own country. By 1861, 11 Southern states had withdrawn from the Union. These states formed their own government and called their country the Confederate States of America.

President Lincoln wanted the United States to stay together. Lincoln ordered Union troops to remain stationed at Fort Sumter in the harbor of Charleston, South Carolina. Southerners believed the fort belonged to the Confederate States. On April 12, 1861, Confederate troops opened fire on Union troops at Fort Sumter. This event started the Civil War (1861–1865).

Some women and children worked in factories during the Civil War. Many of these factories made clothing, blankets, ammunition, and other supplies for the Union Army.

During the Civil War, many slaves ran away from plantations. These contrabands stayed in camps protected by the Union Army.

The Civil War changed the lives of Northern families. Husbands and fathers left their farms and businesses to become soldiers in the Union Army. Women and children took on extra responsibilities. Children often stayed home from school to help with planting and harvesting.

During the Civil War, many factories and businesses that produced supplies for the Union Army thrived. Businesses made ammunition, guns, blankets, uniforms, and other supplies for Union soldiers.

Northerners showed their support for the Union Army by holding rallies and fundraising events. Northerners sometimes held rallies as the Union Army marched through town. Students learned patriotic songs at school to sing at Union rallies.

On April 9, 1865, the Confederacy surrendered, bringing an end to the Civil War. The Union Army helped preserve the United States and brought all states back together as one country.

Send Morse Code Messages

During the Civil War, soldiers used Morse code to send messages by telegraph. This special alphabet was named for Samuel Morse, who invented the telegraph and original code in 1837. Soldiers tapped the long and short signals on one end of a telegraph wire. An electric current produced the same pattern at telegraph stations all along the line. You can write Morse code on paper to send secret messages to your friends.

What You Need

paper and pencil
International Morse Code Chart

What You Do

1. Using the International Morse Code Chart, copy letters to form words and sentences for your message. Be sure to write clearly.
2. Draw a slash line between letters so your friend knows where one letter ends and another begins. Leave a space between words.
3. Be sure your friend has a copy of the code to solve your message.

International Morse Code Chart

A	•–	I	••	R	•–•	1	•––––
B	–•••	K	–•–	S	•••	2	••–––
C	–•–•	L	•–••	T	–	3	•••––
D	–••	M	––	U	••–	4	••••–
E	•	N	–•	V	•••–	5	•••••
F	••–•	O	–––	W	•––	6	–••••
G	––•	P	•––•	X	–••–	7	––•••
H	••••	Q	––•–	Y	–•––	8	–––••
				Z	––••	9	––––•
						10	–––––

Example: ••••/••!   ••••/–––/•–– •–/•–••/•
–•––/–––/••– ?

Message: Hi! How are you?

Schools of the North

During the 1800s, Northern cities grew quickly. Thousands of European immigrants arrived in North America each year. Many of these immigrants settled in cities along the East Coast. By 1860, New York City had more than 1 million residents. In the mid-1800s, children made up more than one-third of the U.S. population. Communities began to organize larger schools for the growing population.

By the start of the Civil War, many different types of schools existed in the North. Most parents sent their children to nearby schools. Some children attended one-room schoolhouses or public schools. Other students enrolled in private academies or boarding schools. Some academies and boarding schools were far away from students' homes.

Northerners who lived in rural farm communities built one-room schoolhouses. A single teacher often taught 10 to 30 students who ranged in age from 4 to 20 years old. All the students sat in the same classroom. Rural teachers taught basic subjects, such as reading, writing, arithmetic, geography, history, spelling, and religion.

Children from wealthy families sometimes attended private academies. These city schools charged a tuition fee based on how many subjects students took and how long they planned to attend. Churches often sponsored academies by donating money and supplies. In academies, teachers often divided boys and girls into separate classrooms or buildings. Academies had smaller classes and more teachers than rural schools. In addition to basic subjects, academies offered classes in music, drawing, dancing, and foreign languages such as Latin and Greek. Some academies offered sewing and manners for girls and navigation for boys who wanted to become sailors.

In the 1820s, cities in New York and Massachusetts began to open free public elementary schools. Prior to this time, most free education was available only to orphans or to very poor children. Money to support the schools came from lotteries, license fees, taxes, and fines. Supporters of public schools believed all children should have the opportunity for a good education, regardless of their family income. By the beginning of the Civil War, public schools existed in most Northern cities.

In one-room schoolhouses, a single teacher often taught children of all ages. In public schools, hundreds of children attended classes in large buildings.

During the Civil War, some boarding schools were opened for war orphans. These children did not have parents who could care for them. Their fathers had died in battle. Some orphans had lost their mothers to illnesses. Widowed women often could not afford to care for their children and sent them to orphan schools.

These boarding schools received money from charitable donations and fundraisers. Some of the money paid for student uniforms, which were similar to the uniforms worn by Union soldiers. During the Civil War, three orphan schools opened in New York. Other states also established orphan schools after the war.

Some Civil War orphans attended Andersonburg School. Boys and girls at this soldiers' orphan school wore uniforms. Students performed marching drills while band members played the fife and drums.

In the 1800s, children did not regularly attend classes. Children in rural areas helped their families with farmwork during planting in the spring and harvesting in the fall. Although some cities had laws that required children to go to school, officials seldom enforced these laws. Many young boys shined shoes or sold newspapers during the day to help the family make extra money. Young girls sometimes worked in clothing mills or sewed homemade items to sell. They had jobs spinning thread or weaving cloth. These children sometimes attended evening or Sunday classes.

Most Americans believed an education was important. Some people wanted their children to learn to read so they could study the Bible. Immigrant families wanted their children to learn the English language. Many families knew that in order for their children to be successful, they needed a basic education.

In the mid-1800s, many children of poor families shined, or polished, shoes before and after school.

Teachers

In the early 1800s, most teachers were men. When the Civil War began, many male teachers joined the army. Schools began to hire single women to teach classes. Women usually quit teaching after they married. Many people felt married women should focus on raising their families.

Rural schools and city schools had different requirements for hiring teachers. Many rural schoolteachers were under 25 years old and taught for only a few years before marrying. Communities paid schoolteachers a salary of about $3 to $5 a week. The community collected taxes to pay for these salaries as well as for school supplies and upkeep of the schoolhouse. In some rural communities, schoolteachers boarded around with families. They lived with a different family each week as part of their salaries.

Most male academy and public schoolteachers planned to make a career as a teacher. Teachers in city schools often taught just one age group. Schoolteachers in public schools or academies earned a salary of about $5 to $15 per week.

In the mid-1800s, many teachers trained at normal schools. These training schools provided courses in subjects teachers would teach to their students. Normal schools also trained schoolteachers how to organize and present lessons.

Charlotte Forten was a free African American teacher from the North. During the Civil War, Charlotte taught escaped slaves in South Carolina.

In 1865, this group of Northern schoolteachers taught newly freed slaves.

Teachers taught lessons in 15- to 30-minute recitations. These reading or lecture reviews tested students' knowledge. Students performed recitations individually and as a group. Some recitations were question-and-answer tests. The teacher asked a student a question, and the student responded with the answer. During other recitations, children repeated memorized lessons, passages from books, or compositions. Teachers also spent time explaining the subjects during recitations.

During noon recess, children ate lunch and played games with classmates. Most children brought lunches from home in empty lard containers. These round, metal pails had lids to keep the food covered. The pails also had handles, which made them easy to carry to and from school. Because many children used similar lunch pails, parents often tied scraps of cloth or yarn to the handle so children knew which lunch was theirs.

Grammar school students took examinations during the school year to show parents and community members what they had learned. Many schools held examination sessions twice a year—once in the winter and once in the spring. Other schools held a final examination only in the spring.

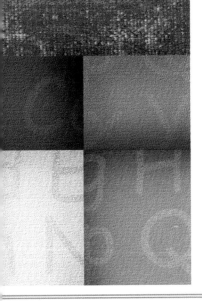

After eating lunch, boys and girls played games on the playground such as hoops, hopscotch, marbles (below), and jump rope.

Playing Hoops

Hoops has been a popular outdoor game for centuries. Rolling a hoop takes practice. You can play hoops alone, race a friend, or have team relay races. You will need help from an adult to make your hoop stick.

What You Need

one hula hoop
one length of wood, 12 inches (30 centimeters) long, 1 inch
   (2.5 centimeters) wide, and 1 inch (2.5 centimeters) thick

one length of wood, 36 inches (1 meter) long, 1 inch
   (2.5 centimeters) wide, and 1 inch (2.5 centimeters) thick
two nails
hammer

What You Do

1. Stand the long length of wood on end. Place the short length of wood across the top of the long length of wood, centering the long piece underneath it. The two pieces of wood should form a T. Pound nails through the short piece of wood to connect the two pieces. This is the hoop stick.

2. Decide how far you want to race your hoop. Racing around a tree or in curved lines is more difficult.

3. To start, hold the hoop stick by the long handle, placing the cross of the T on the ground. Tip the stick forward to make a ramp with the T. Roll the hoop down the tilted T to get it rolling.

4. Use the stick like a mallet to tap the back of the hoop. Some players push the inside of the hoop with one end of the T to keep the hoop rolling. Practice rolling your hoop before you start the race. If your hoop falls over, you must start again.

5. The first person to finish the race wins.

In 1861, free African American children attended this orphan school in New York.

Teachers organized the examinations and quizzed students on all of their school subjects. Children recited poems, read essays, and solved arithmetic problems as part of their examinations. If students were successful during their examinations, they passed to the next grade.

African Americans attended separate schools. These schools often were established by African Americans or church groups. African American schools did not receive much funding. They did not have as many supplies as public schools. Teachers often held classes in rundown buildings.

Free African Americans

Most African Americans who lived in Northern states were free. Many white people in the North were abolitionists who thought that slavery was wrong. But many also believed that African Americans were inferior to white people. These Northerners thought African Americans did not deserve equal opportunities. For this reason, most restaurants, shops, train cars, schools, and other public facilities were segregated. African Americans had to sit, stand, and shop in areas that were separate from white people. African Americans sometimes even had to use separate entrances and exits.

Most white people did not want their children to go to school with African American children. African Americans opened their own schools. These schools did not have much money. Students studied from used books, handed down from white public schools.

African American schools sometimes closed down when funding and supplies ran out.

African Americans who could not afford to send all of their children to school sometimes sent a different child each day. In the evenings, brothers and sisters taught each other.

An African American schoolteacher gives a lesson on objects.

Studying during the Civil War

During the Civil War, children studied reading, writing, and spelling from *McGuffey's Readers*. These textbooks contained lessons for different grade levels. The advanced readers included lessons in geography and history. As students reached the higher grades, they recited essays from their readers by memory.

Students solved arithmetic problems at their desks on slates. Children wrote with chalk on these small slate boards. Later, they erased their work with a damp cloth and reused the slates. Teachers often had the entire class race to see who could solve an arithmetic problem the fastest.

In the 1800s, penmanship was an important school subject. Students practiced penmanship using quill pens and ink. Teachers taught students how to hold the pen, place the paper, and precisely form letters. They also taught children the correct posture to use while writing. In the 1800s, teachers forced children to write with their right hand. Students practiced their writing skills by copying words and phrases from penmanship copybooks. Because all students learned from the same copybooks, many children had similar handwriting styles.

Children quietly walked in and out of classrooms in orderly lines. At times, students entered the school while the teacher played music on the piano.

After the Civil War started, book publishers began printing school textbooks that encouraged children to support the Union Army. Young girls and boys learned the alphabet and simple reading lessons from *The Union ABC*. Many lessons in this book focused on loyalty to the Union and moral values. *The Union ABC* included rhymes such as "O is an Officer, proud of his station. P is the President, who rules this great nation."

Some children read magazines such as School Fellow Magazine *and* The Little Corporal. *These magazines often contained patriotic stories and poems.*

School assignments often centered on patriotism. Daily music lessons in some schools included songs such as "The Star-Spangled Banner," "America," or "Rally 'Round the Flag." Reading assignments included stories about Abraham Lincoln. Teachers assigned composition topics on bravery and duty to the Union. Many children chose to perform oral recitations of poems and essays about the war. A favorite poem was "Sheridan's Ride," based on the Battle of Cedar Creek.

Some schools sponsored special events to encourage people to support the Union. Local politicians gave rousing speeches, while schoolchildren sang patriotic songs at flag-raising ceremonies. At pageants, people sang Union songs and groups of boys performed military drills they learned at school. Students wrote and presented original plays that featured brave soldiers and the loyal family members who supported them.

Rallying Song

A band plays patriotic songs during a Union rally.

Schoolchildren sometimes sang rallying songs during the school day. Union soldiers and Northerners also sang these inspiring songs as soldiers marched through town or when they left for battle. One popular rallying song was "Rally 'Round the Flag."

Oh, we'll rally 'round the flag, boys,

Rally once again,

Shouting the battle cry of freedom.

We will rally from the hillside,

Gather from the plain,

Shouting the battle cry of freedom.

Chorus

The Union forever, hurrah, boys, hurrah!

Down with the traitor and up with the star!

While we rally 'round the flag boys,

Rally once again,

Shouting the battle cry of freedom.

Union Loyalty and Support

Since most Civil War battles were fought in the South, few towns in the North were harmed. But the Civil War affected Northern children in many other ways. Many fathers, brothers, and cousins enlisted in the army. Families anxiously read war bulletins printed in newspapers or posted at telegraph offices. These announcements gave battle reports and lists of soldiers who had been wounded or killed. Many soldiers died during battle or from disease and illness. Some soldiers returned from the war missing an arm or a leg.

Mothers expected children to help with daily household chores while other family members were away at war. Farm children carried wood, built fires, milked and fed cows, worked in the garden, and washed dishes. They sometimes cared for younger brothers and sisters and helped with laundry. In cities, some women began working in factories and mills as more men left these jobs to enlist as soldiers. City children helped at home with cooking, cleaning, and caring for younger siblings. Some children also held part-time jobs to help support their families.

Children also helped support the Union Army. They sent packages and letters to relatives who were away at war. Soldiers often wrote back to family members about their experiences. Families and church groups gathered to sew clothing, knit socks

Some younger boys ran away from home or signed up to become drummer boys or buglers for Union regiments. These drummer boys served the 61st New York Infantry in 1863 (left). Children studied from books that supported the Union Army (below).

and mittens, and prepare food items to send to soldiers. During these drives, people read letters from soldiers out loud. Northern children also raised more than $16,000 for the Union selling photographs of President Lincoln. The Union Army awarded children military ranks and prizes based on the number of photos they sold.

During the Civil War, thousands of boys in their early- to mid-teens joined the Union Army. Some estimates say that more than 40,000 drummer boys served in the Union Army. Some boys lied about their age to enlist as drummer boys, buglers, or even soldiers. They wanted to be a part of the war and have a chance to serve the Union. Older soldiers called boy soldiers "ponies."

Northern communities held fairs sponsored by the U.S. Sanitary Commission. This government agency was established in 1861 to monitor the diet and health of troops and to organize military hospitals. Many children's booths sold cakes, pies, jams,

27

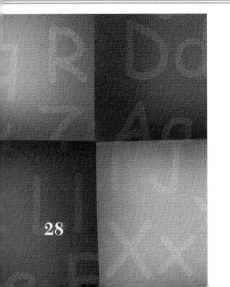

After the war, the Freedmen's Bureau opened the Abraham Lincoln School for free African Americans in New Orleans, Louisiana.

embroidered towels, or other homemade items. The funds raised from these sales went to the U.S. Sanitary Commission and the war effort. These fairs raised $4.3 million to provide food and medical supplies for Union soldiers.

After the Civil War, the government worked to set up a system of schools to educate freed African Americans. Many Northern churches and charities provided the money to build schools and to buy supplies in the South. Organizations such as the Institute for Colored Youth trained African American men and women as teachers. In 1865, the government formed the Freedmen's Bureau. This agency helped build schools and provide teachers for African Americans in the South.

After the Confederacy surrendered, the United States faced the problem of bringing the states together into one country again. The time of rebuilding was called Reconstruction. It lasted from 1865 to 1877. In the South, many homes, town buildings, and plantations had to be repaired or rebuilt. Many people also worked to rebuild their families. Soldiers returned after months or years away from their loved ones. Other families had to learn to survive without fathers, sons, and brothers who died during the war.

Hold a Penny Drive

Many children in the North participated in fundraising events to support Union soldiers during the Civil War. You can hold your own fundraiser to support a local charity or hospital or to buy books for your school library. This activity can be a great community service project for your school. You will need a teacher or other adult to help organize your penny drive.

What You Need

poster paper and colored pens or crayons to make
   advertising posters

one or more large, clear jars to hold pennies

Bring in Your Pennies!

Help support our local Salvation Army

What You Do

1. With your teacher and class, choose a local group for a penny drive. Your teacher should contact this group to be sure they do not have special rules about accepting donations.
2. Set a start date and an end date for the penny drive. One week usually is plenty of time.
3. Invite other classes to join you in the penny drive. You could hold a contest to see which class brings the most pennies.
4. Each class needs its own penny jar. Ask at your school kitchen to see if they have any empty clear glass or plastic jars you could use.
5. Create colorful posters to place around your school to remind people to bring pennies.
6. During the week of the penny drive, encourage everyone to bring in some pennies. Place the pennies in the jar and watch it fill up during the week.
7. On the last day of the penny drive, each class should count their pennies. Your teacher should double-check the total. Compare classes to see who brought the most pennies. Add all the class totals together for a grand-total amount.
8. Your teacher should arrange for the money to be donated to the organization you chose.

Words to Know

abolitionist (ab-uh-LISH-uh-nist)—someone who worked to end slavery before the Civil War

facility (fuh-SIL-uh-tee)—an area or building in a community provided for people to use, such as a theater, park, or shop

inferior (in-FIHR-ee-ur)—not as good as or not equal to something or someone else

pageant (PAJ-uhnt)—a public show where people act out stories

patriotic (pay-tree-AH-tik)—loyal to a country

recitation (ress-i-TAY-shuhn)—a lesson spoken out loud to a teacher

rural (RUR-uhl)—an area in the countryside or outside of the city

segregated (SEG-ruh-gat-ed)—separated according to race

siblings (SIB-lings)—brothers or sisters

urban (UR-buhn)—a city area

To Learn More

Bircher, William. *A Civil War Drummer Boy: The Diary of William Bircher, 1861–1865.* Diaries, Letters, and Memoirs. Mankato, Minn.: Blue Earth Books, 2000.

Forten, Charlotte. Edited by Christy Steele with Kerry Graves. *A Free Black Girl before the Civil War: The Diary of Charlotte Forten, 1854.* Mankato, Minn.: Blue Earth Books, 2000.

Herbert, Janis. *The Civil War for Kids: A History with 21 Activities.* Chicago: Chicago Review Press, 1999.

Marten, James Alan, Editor. *Lessons of War: The Civil War in Children's Magazines.* Wilmington, Del.: SR Books, 1999.

Wroble, Lisa A. *Kids During the American Civil War.* Kids Throughout History. New York: PowerKids Press, 1997.

Internet Sites

The American Civil War Home Page
http://sunsite.utk.edu/civil-war

Boys in the Civil War
http://www.civilwarhome.com/boysinwar.htm

Children of the 1860s
http://www.geocities.com/Athens/Delphi/7194/child.html

The Civil War
http://www.civilwar.com

Fort Ward Museum Kid's Page
http://ci.alexandria.va.us/oha/fortward/fw-kids.html

The Ohio Village
http://www.ohiohistory.org/places/ohvillage

Places to Visit

Fort Ward Museum and Historic Site
4301 West Braddock Road
Alexandria, VA 22304

Gettysburg National Military Park
97 Taneytown Road
Gettysburg, PA 17325

Harford Historical Society & The Soldiers Orphan School
Orphan School Road
Harford, PA 18823

Old Stone School
732 North Main Street
Lanesboro, MA 01237

Index

DATE DUE
